Gravures
Par
Michel Le Blon

Engravings
of
Michel Le Blon

Edited by
Robert L. Angus

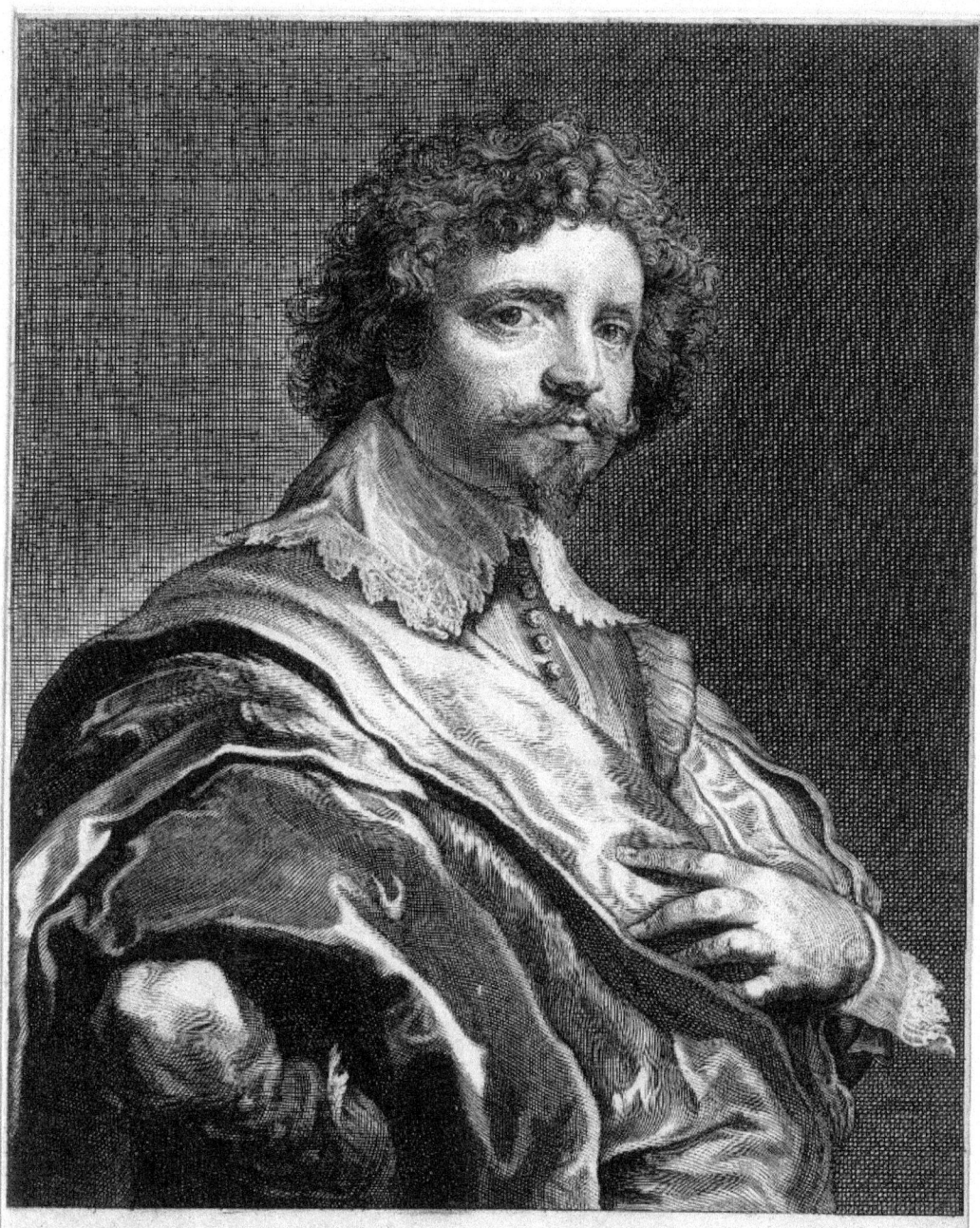

Michel le Blon Agent
de la Royne et Couronne de Suede
chez sa Ma.té de la Grande Bretagne

MICHEL LE BLON: (*bapt* Frankfurt am Main, 9 July 1587; *d* Amsterdam, 1656). German goldsmith and engraver, active in the Netherlands and England. He was of Huguenot descent and trained as a goldsmith but was already active as an engraver in 1605, the date of his earliest-known engravings (London, BM) of grotesque ornament suitable for jewellery. He may have studied under Theodor de Bry and Johann Theodor de Bry. Le Blon probably settled in Amsterdam in about 1610.

His *Eenvoldige vruchten en spitsen voor d'ancomen kunst liefhebbende ieucht* was published in 1611, comprising 14 plates of ornament for goldsmiths' work: borders and friezes, with exotic birds, animals, insects, fish, flowers, vegetables, fruits and leaves. He also published engravings for the decoration of knife-handles and sword-handles, as well as heraldic shields and mantling for engraving on silver and some almost Auricular-style strapwork designs. In 1627 he issued a collection of engraved shields, emblems and small pictorial scenes, some religious, for the decoration of box-lids and watches. In the same year he travelled to Italy, possibly with Joachim van Sandrart.

Le Blon also spent many years in England as an agent of the Swedish court and frequently visited Stockholm in this capacity. An English tankard (*c.* 1620-30; London, V&A) bears one of his designs.

He signed his work *Blondus, Micha?l Blondus* or with a monogram of the letters M and B.

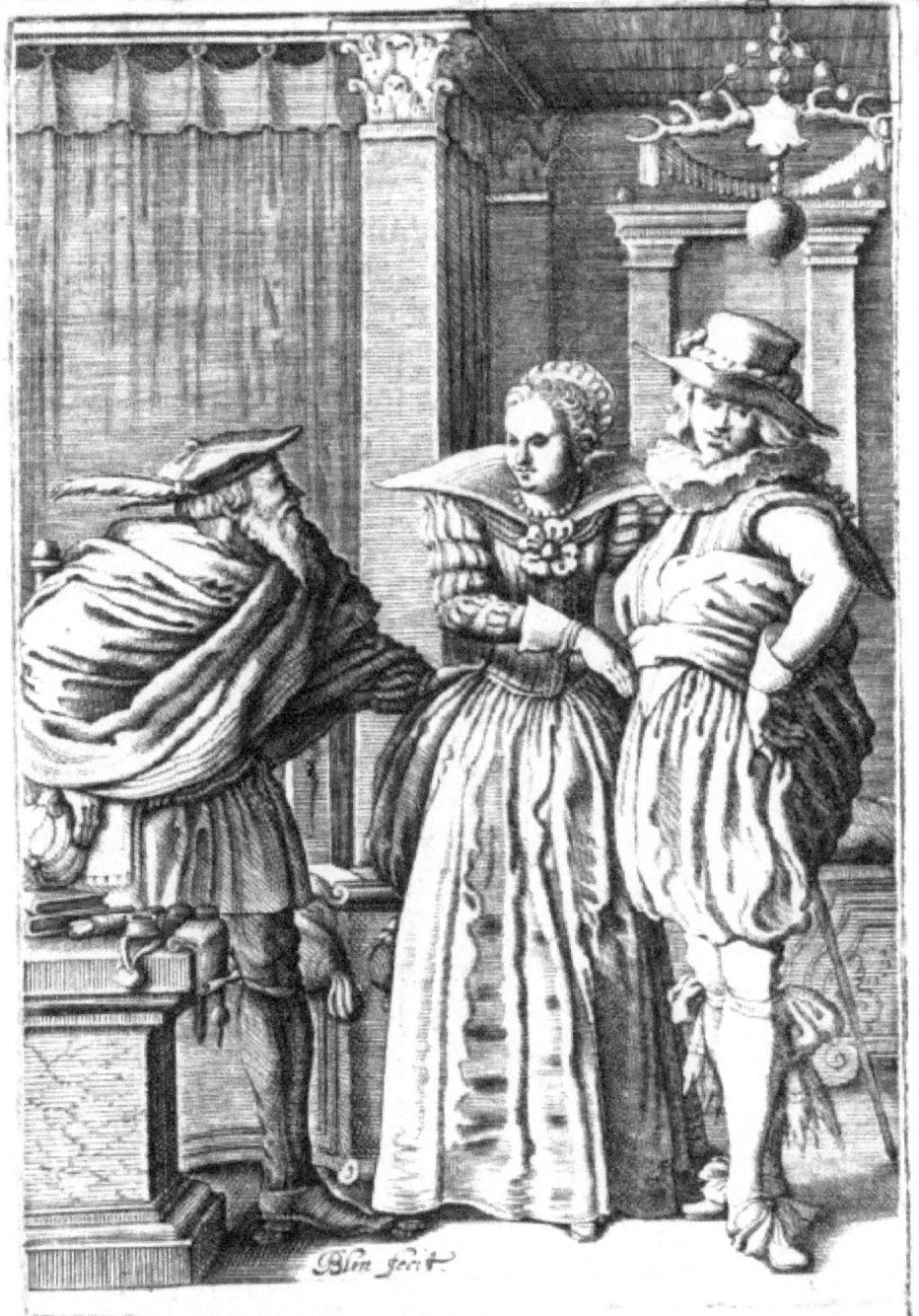

Blan fecit.

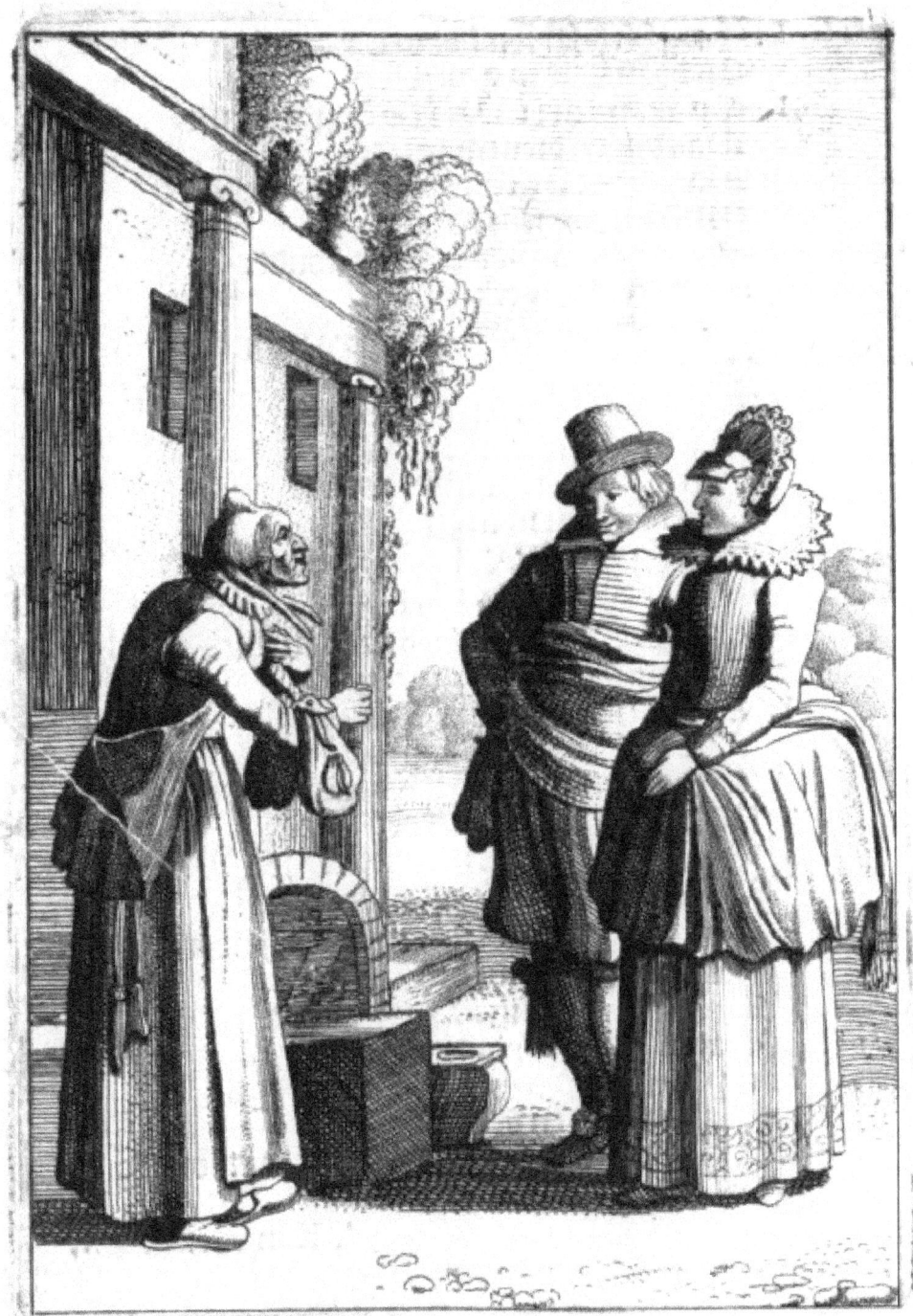

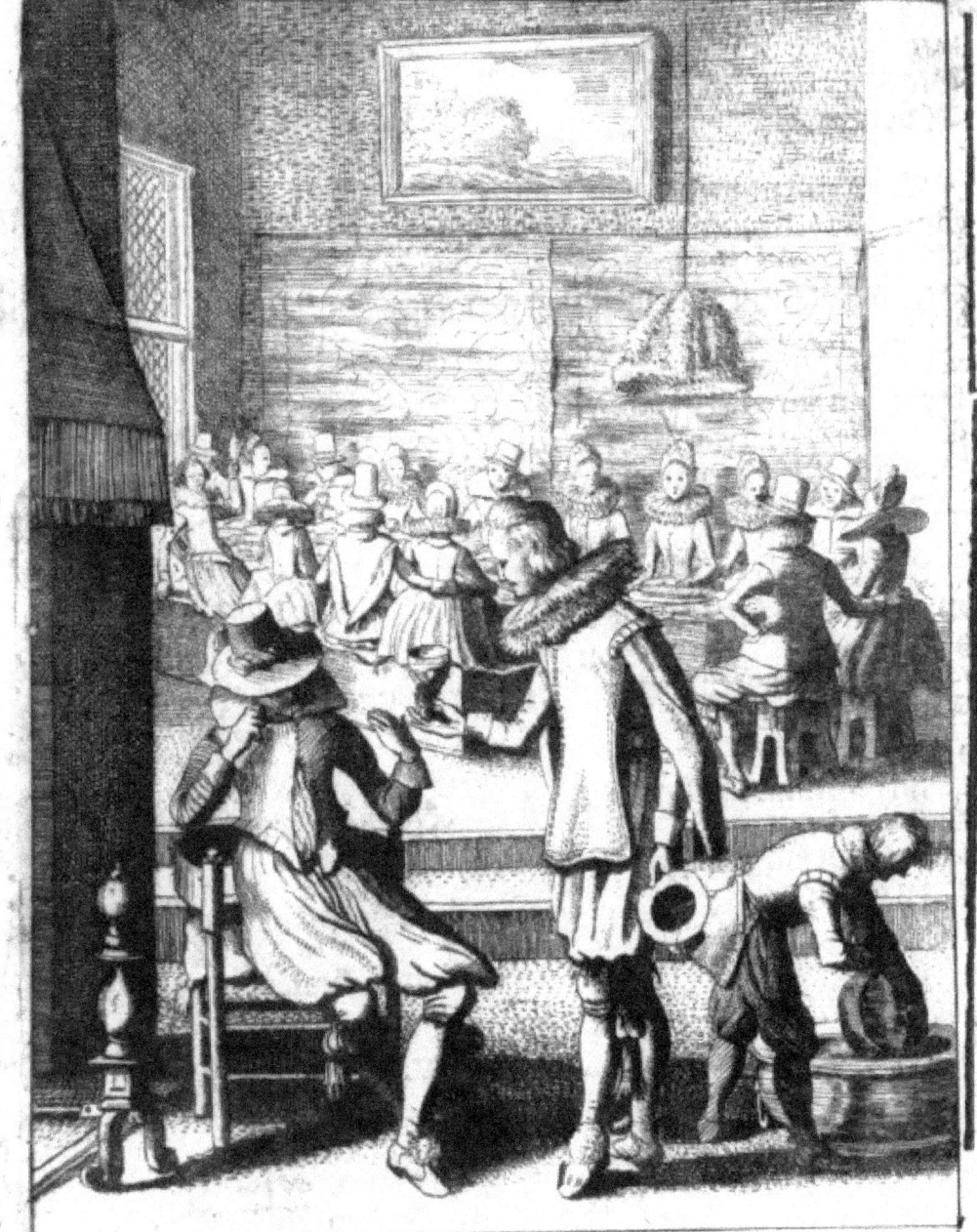

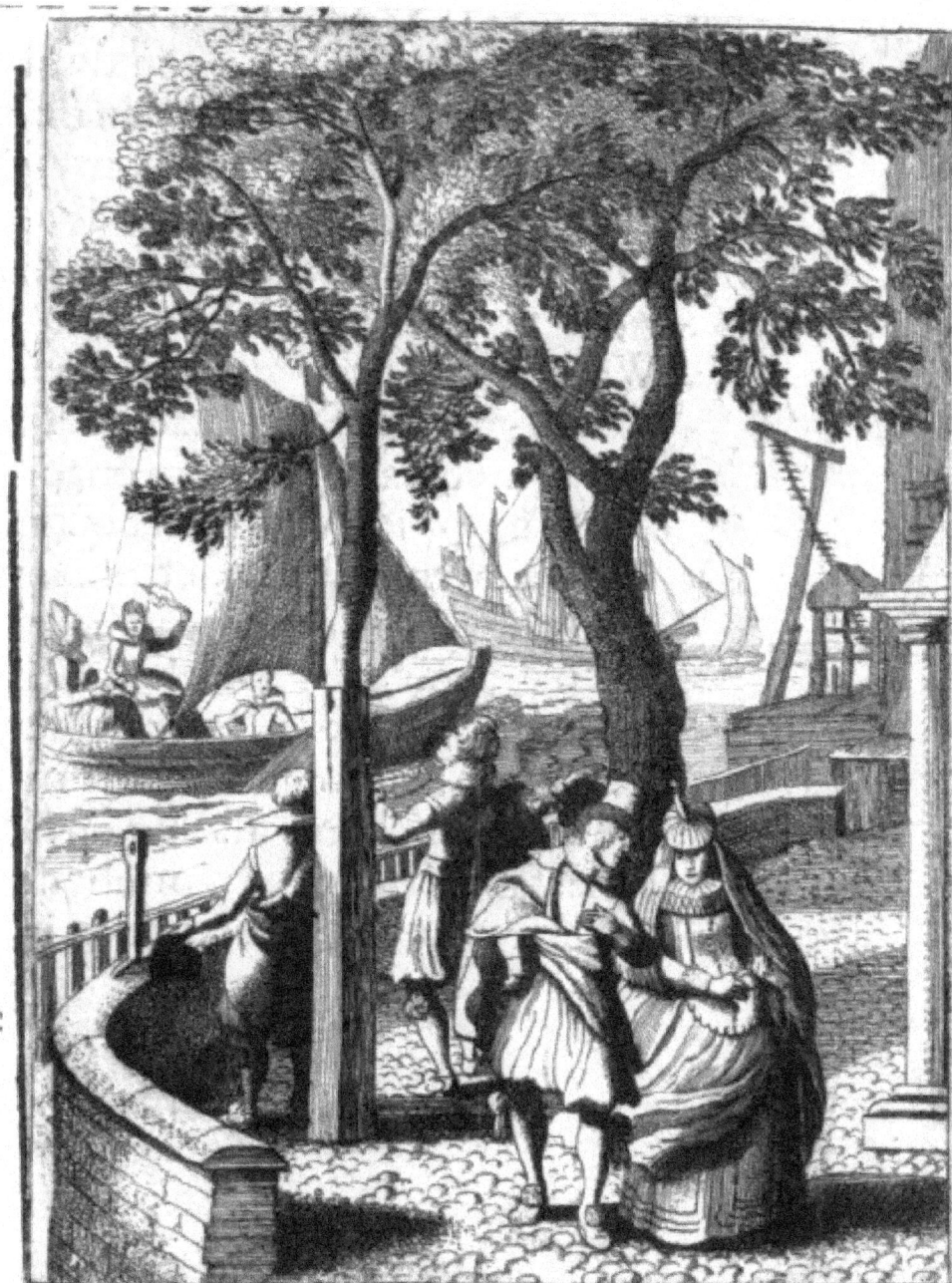

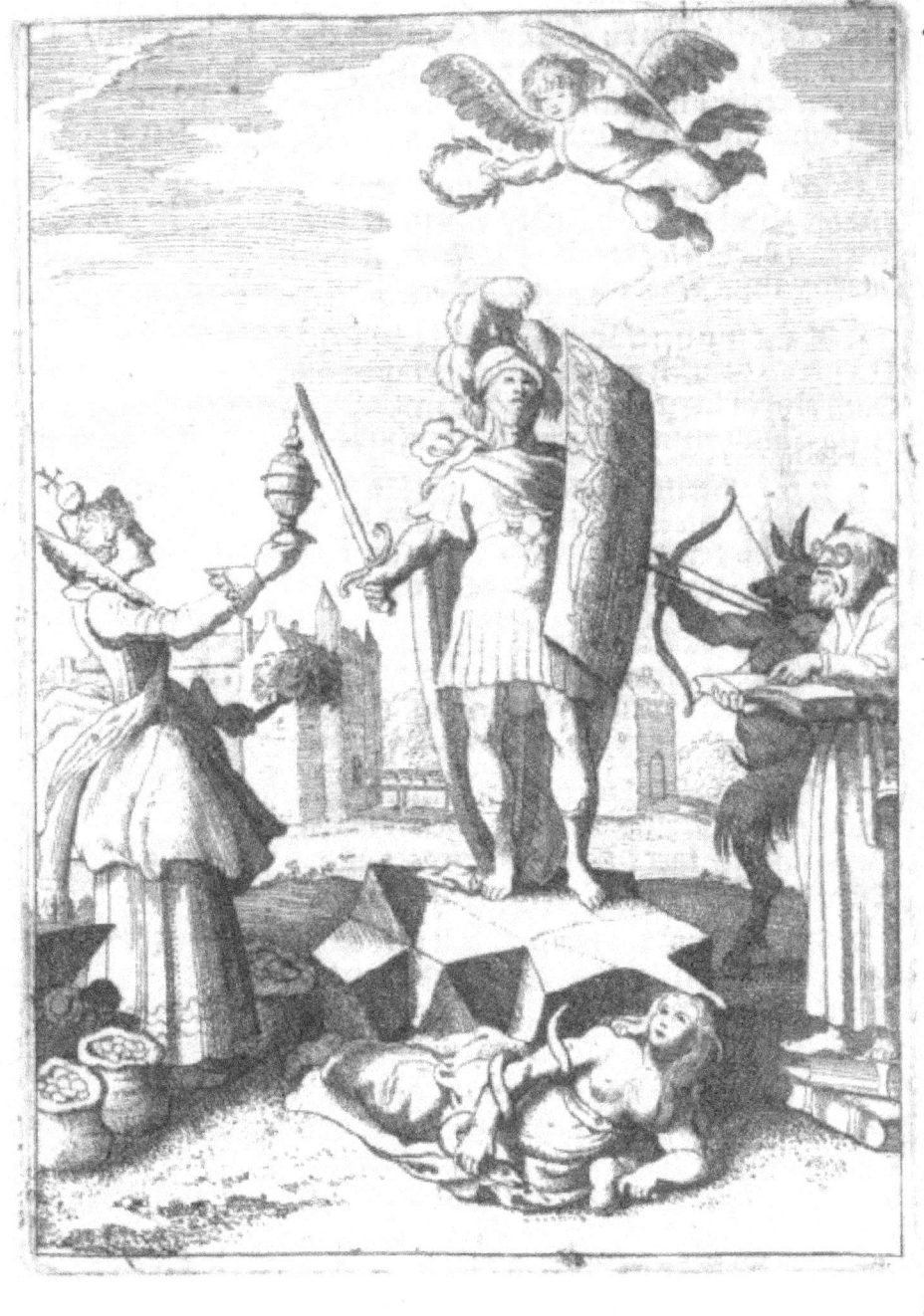

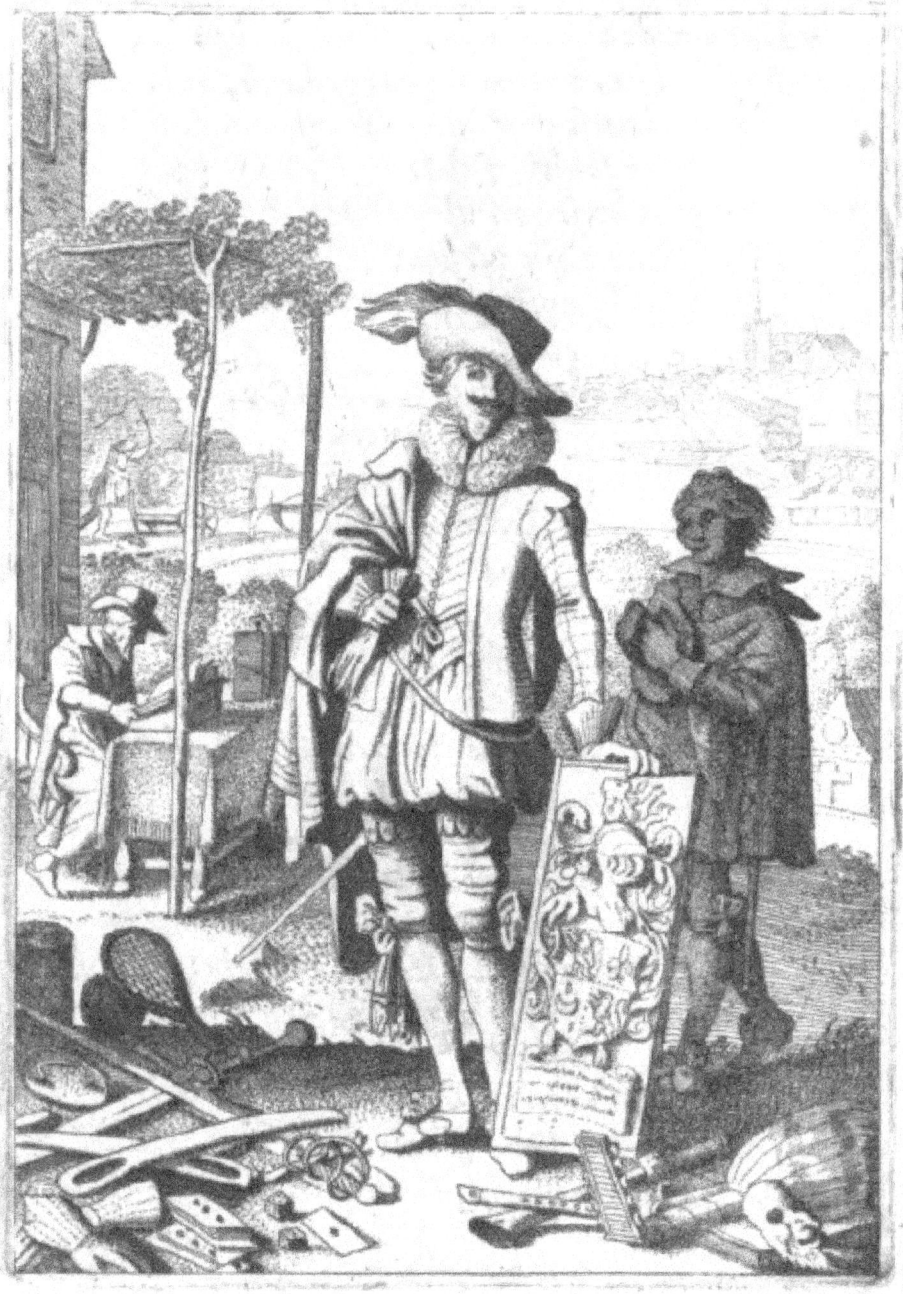

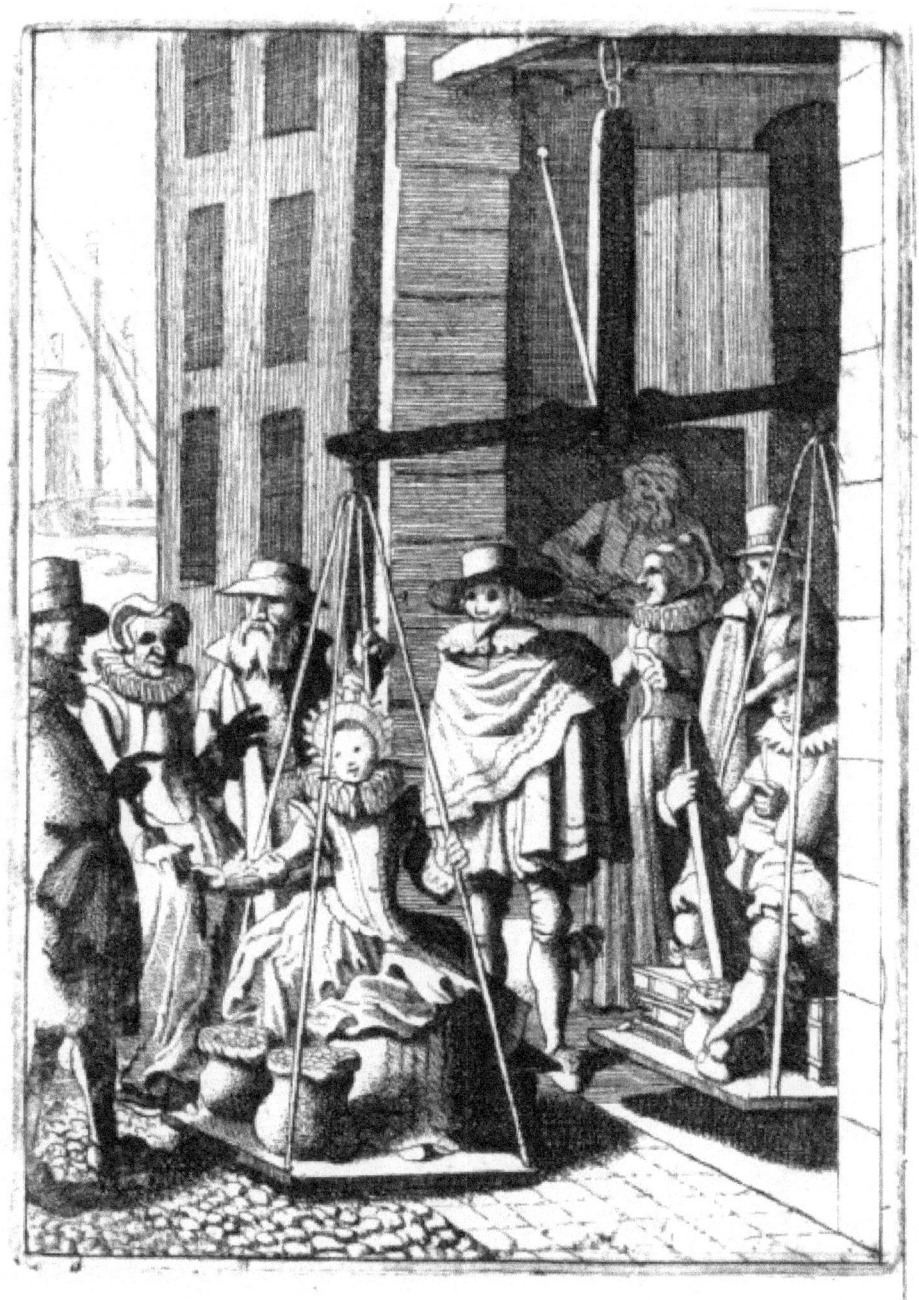

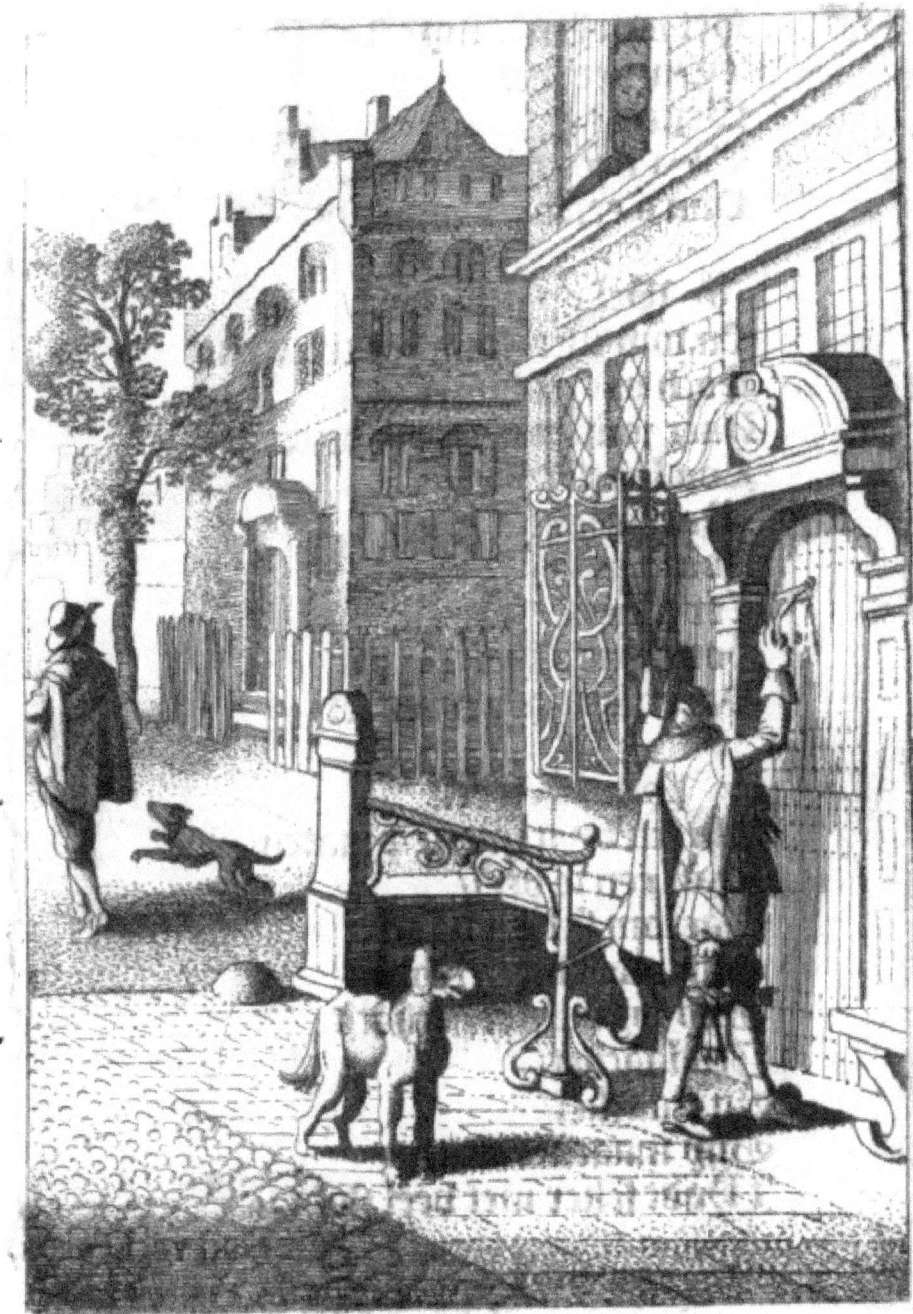

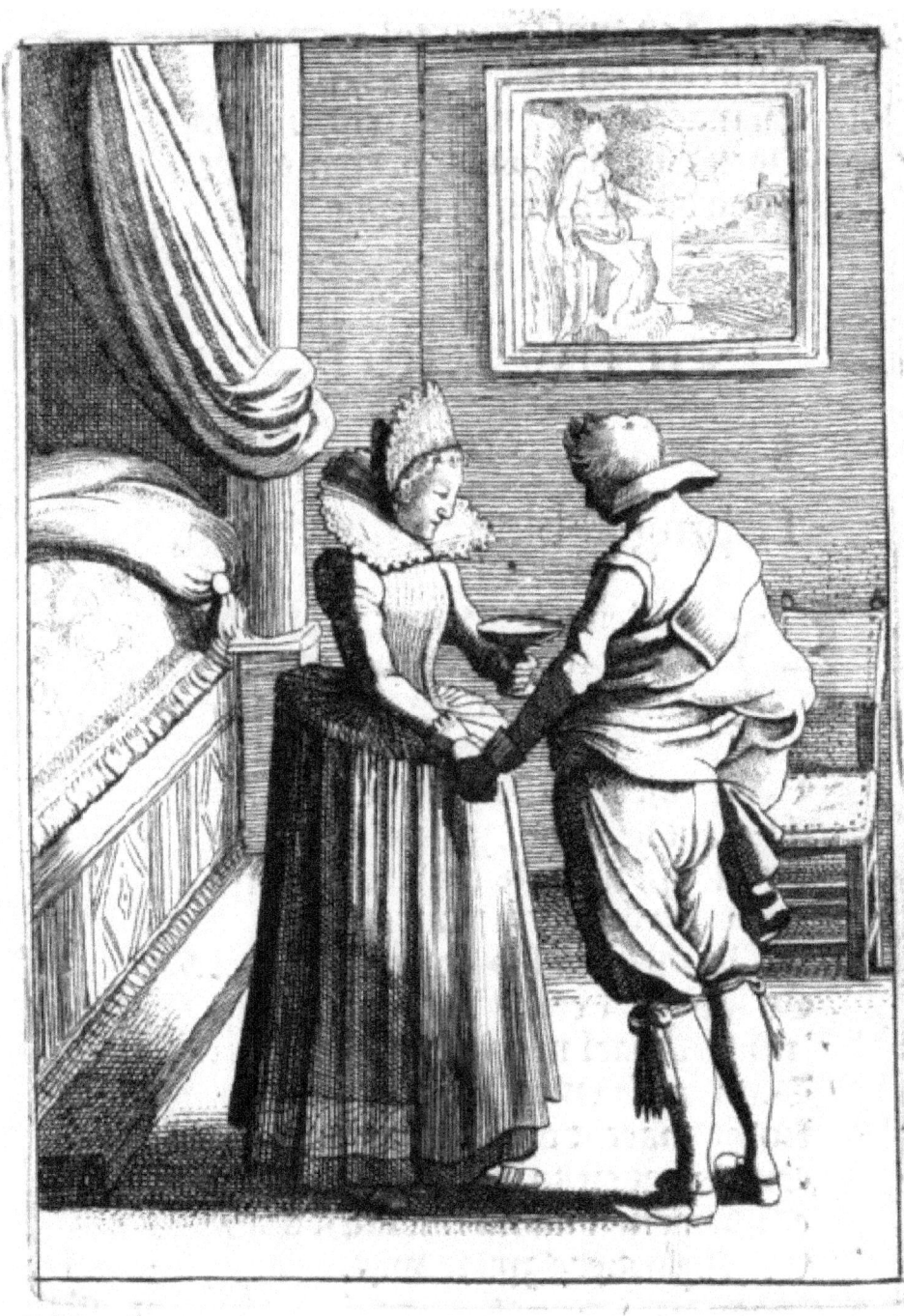

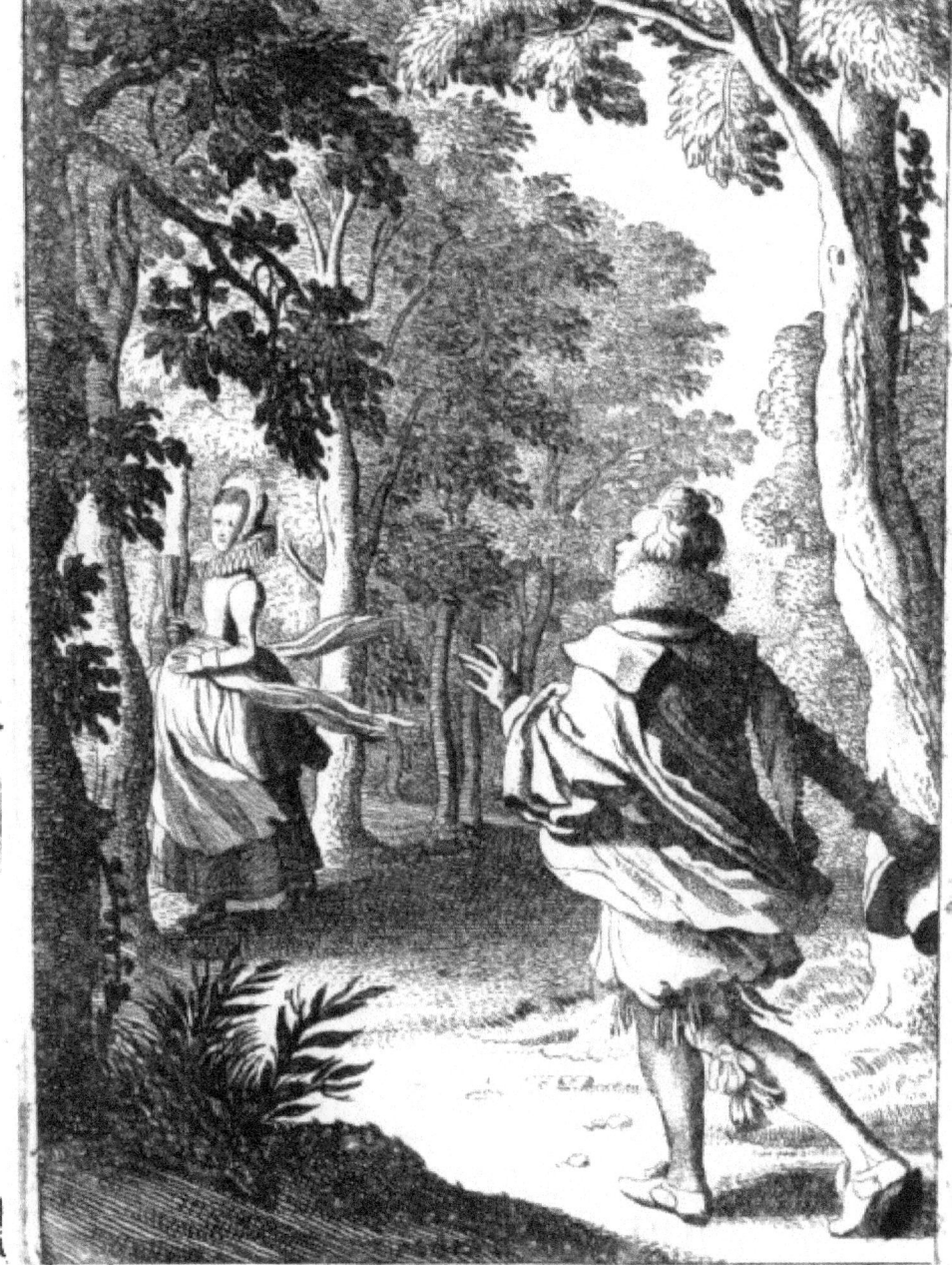

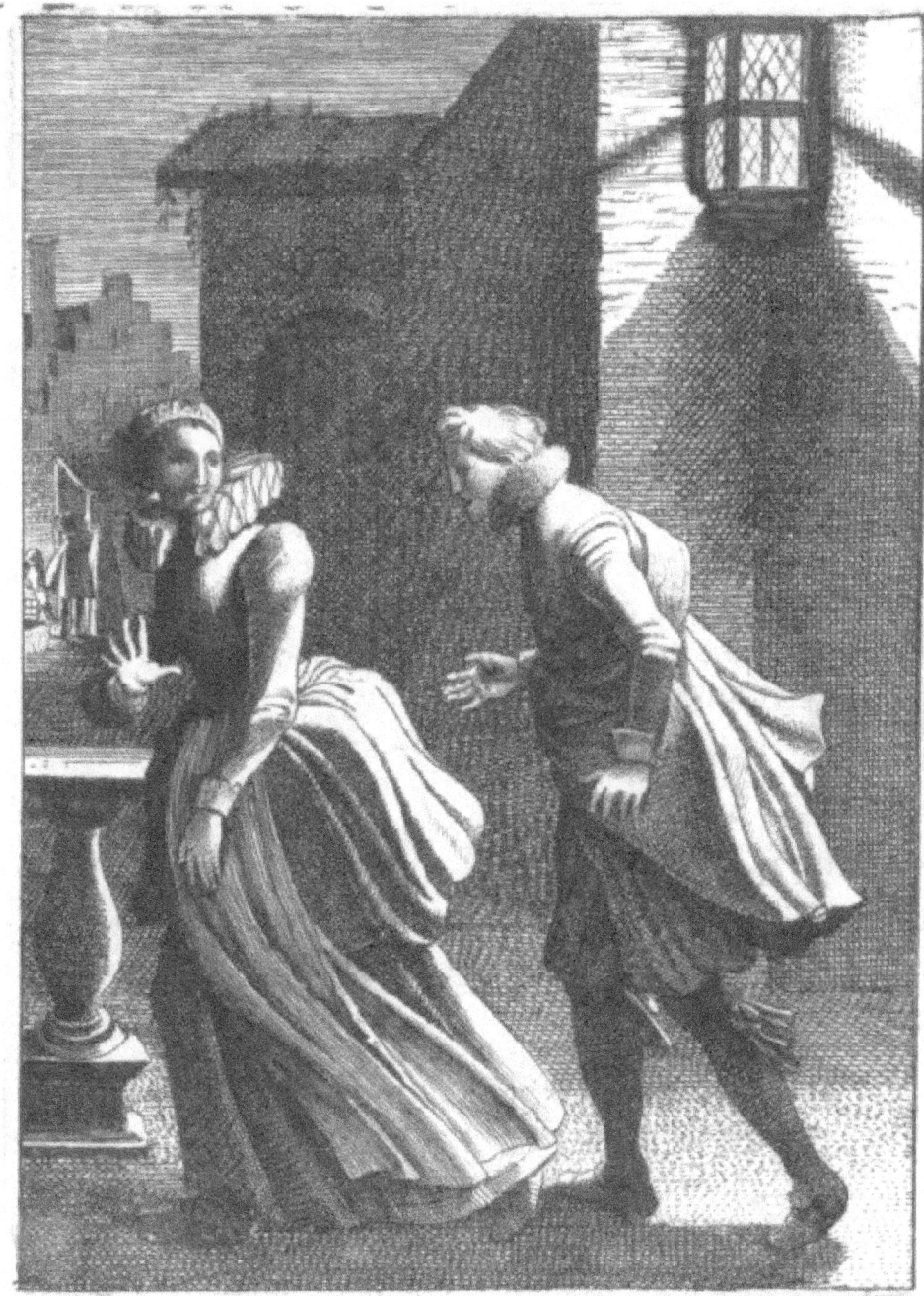

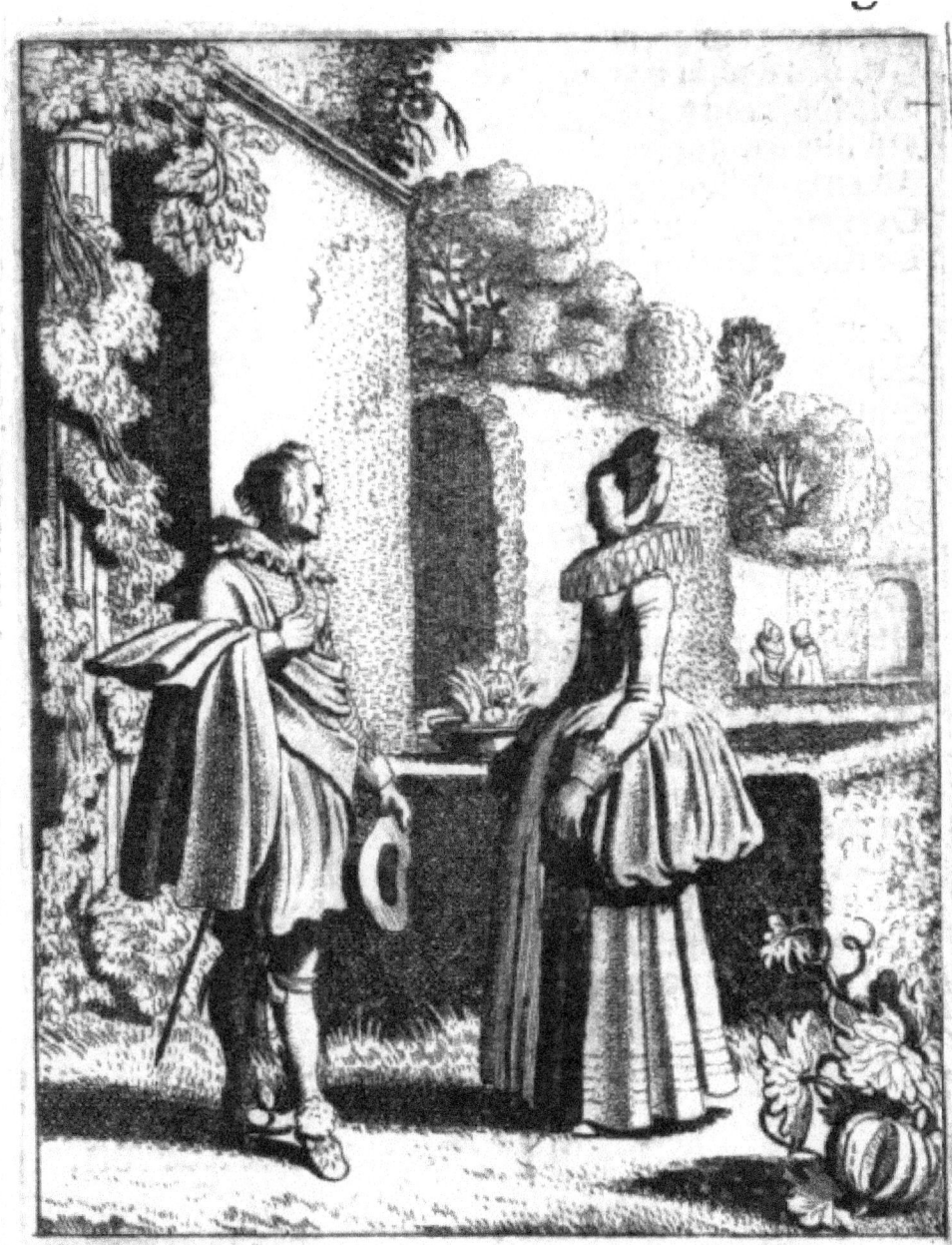

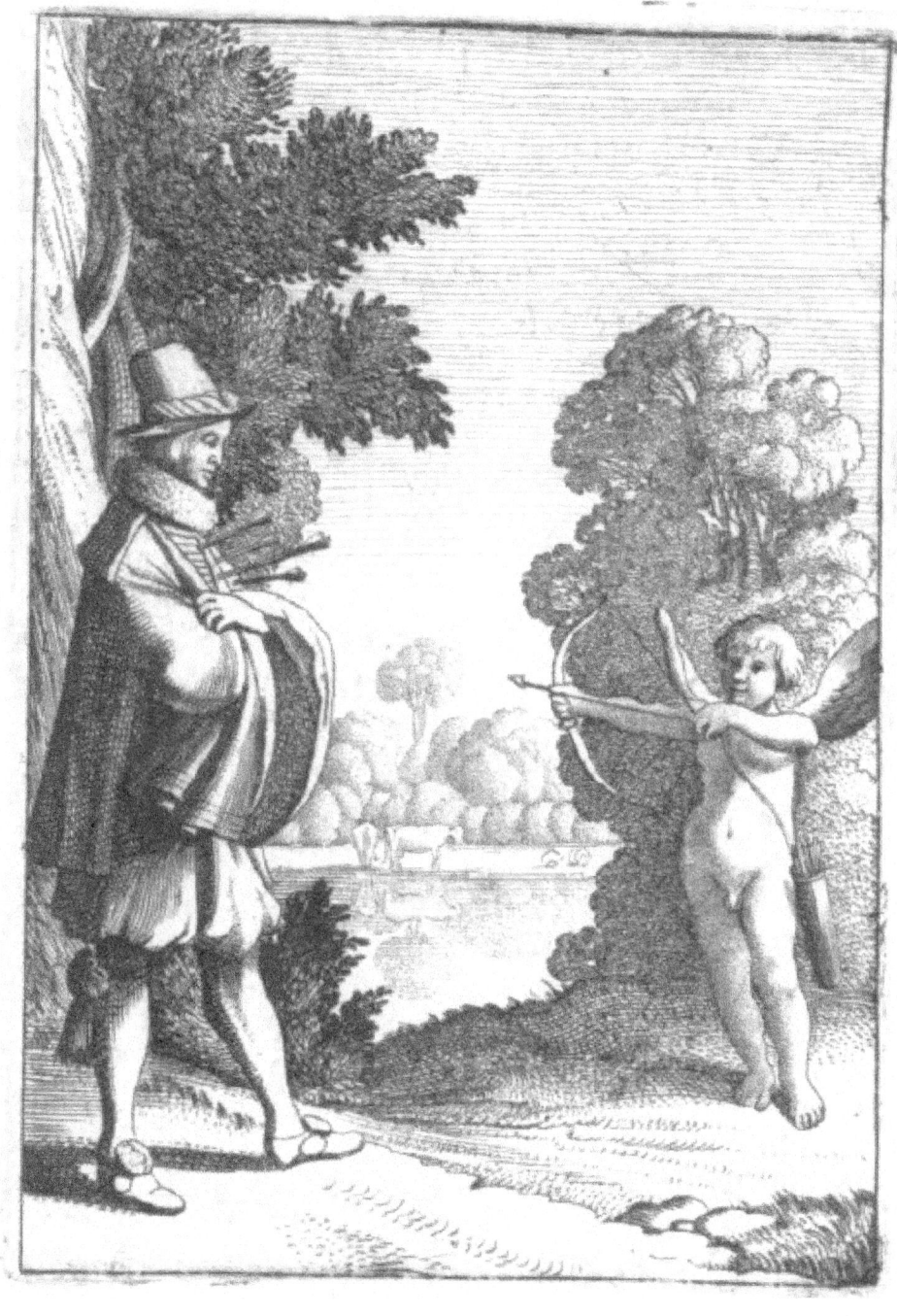

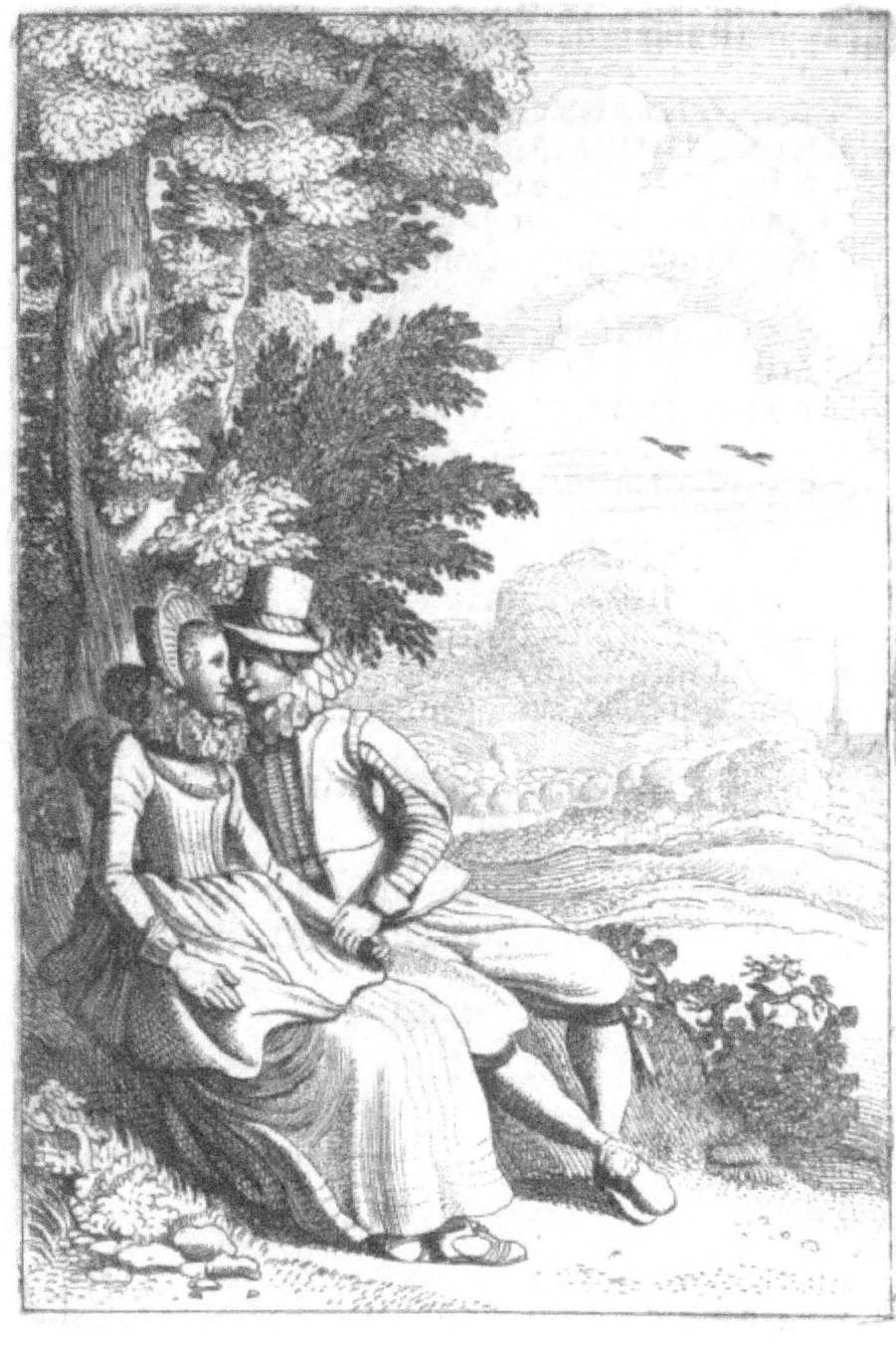

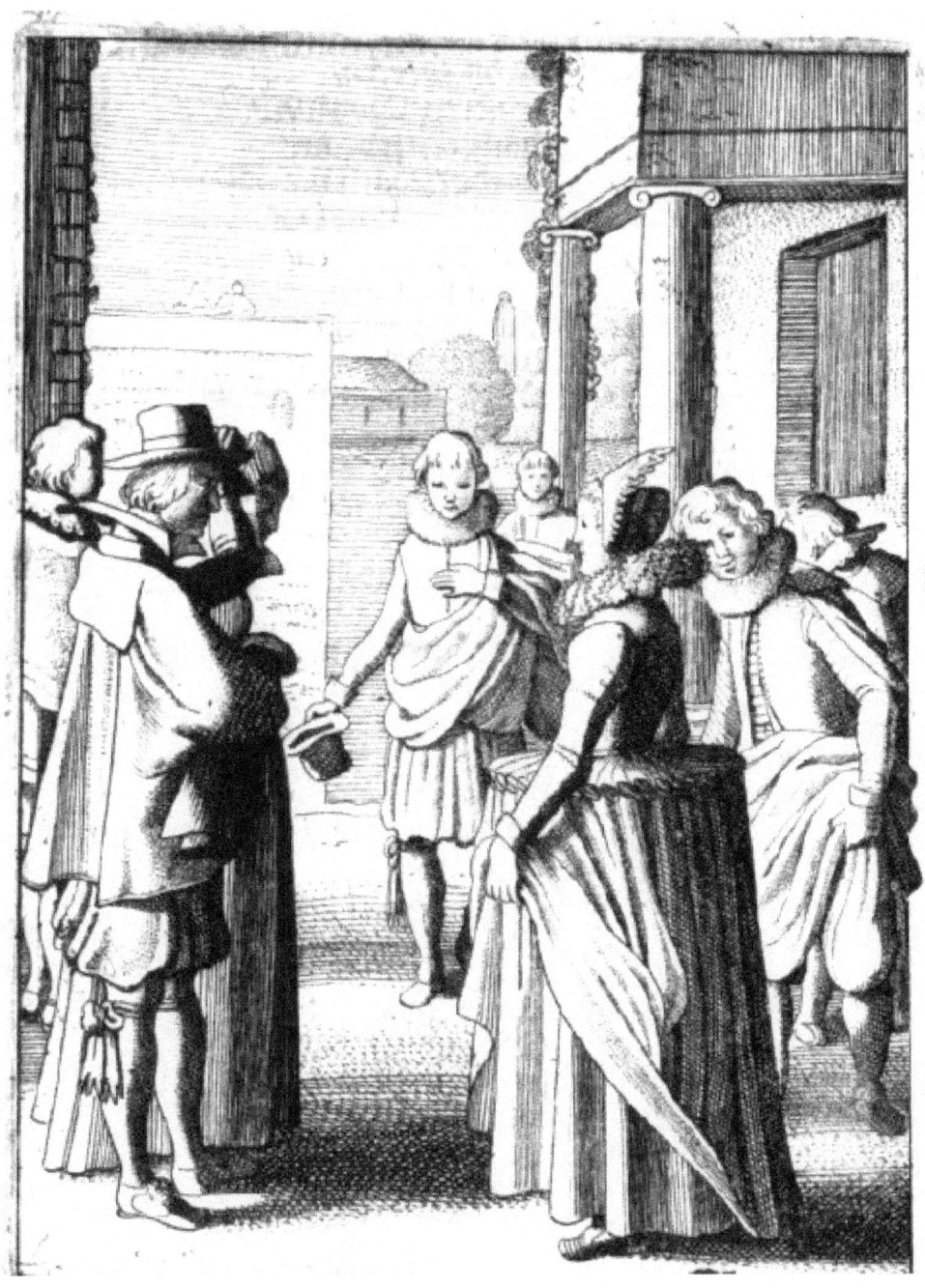

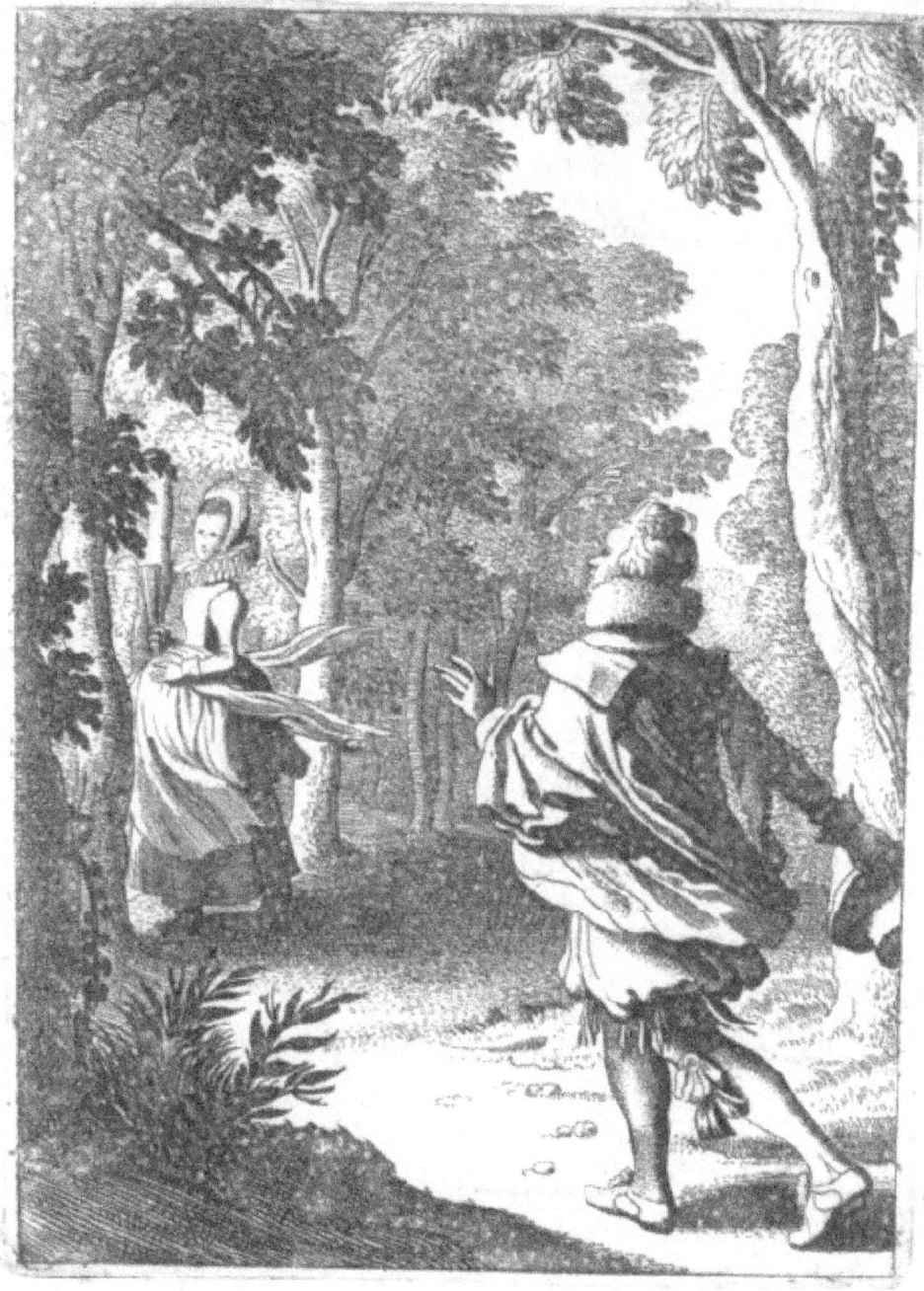

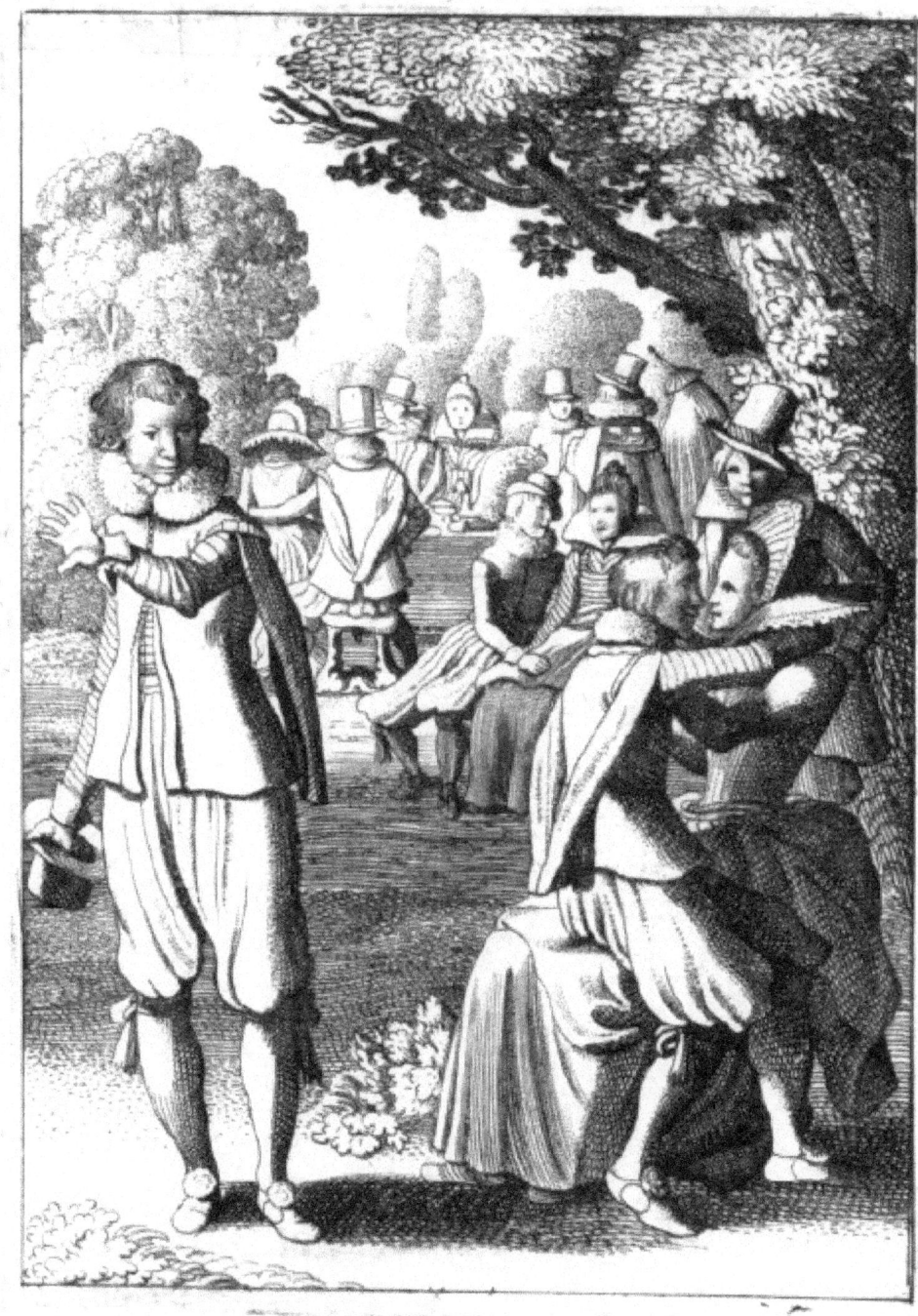

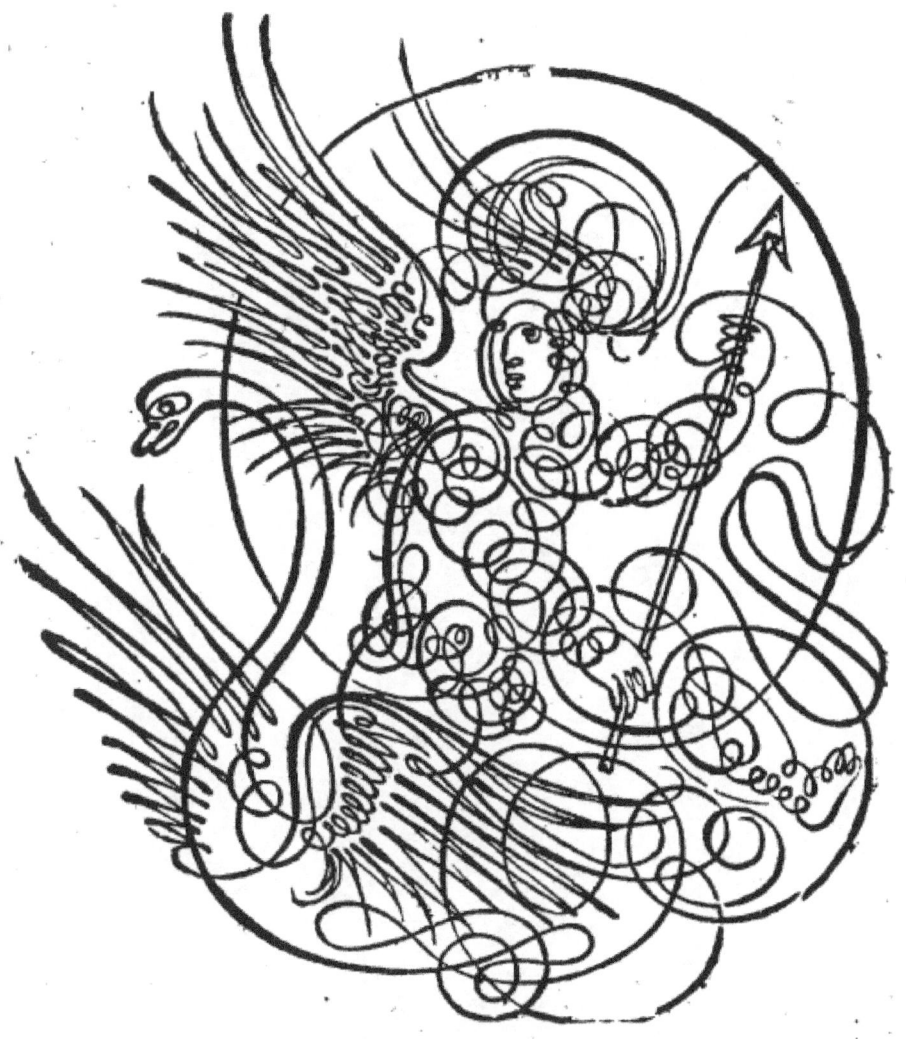

Cupido reyst van hier ghy zyt hier niet bescheyden,
V krachten zijn hier dof, ghy zyt hier onbekent.
De GOD, der trouwen GOD vereenighde haar beyden
Met Liefde. Niet met Min, die qualijck loont int ent.

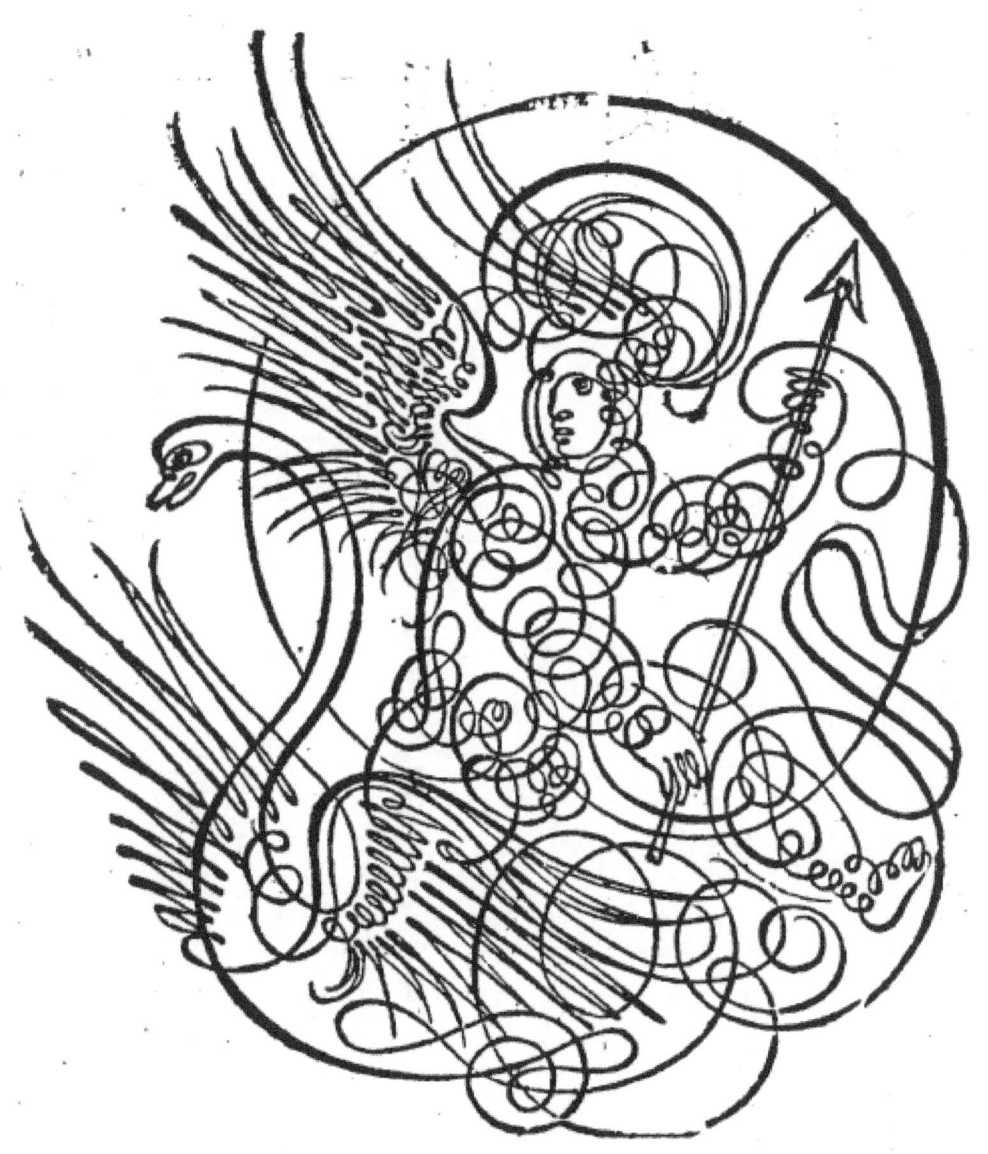

Swaen-Ridder, geyl, en blindt, ghy moet van hier vertrecken,
Hier hebdy niet te doen, want dit geliefde Paer
Dat heeft die goede God met wijsheydt gaan verwecken,
En met zijn Liefde voort vereenight met melkaer.

www.ingramcontent.com/pod-product-compliance
Lightning Source LLC
Chambersburg PA
CBHW071547170526
45166CB00004B/1577